CODES OF PUBLIC SLEEP

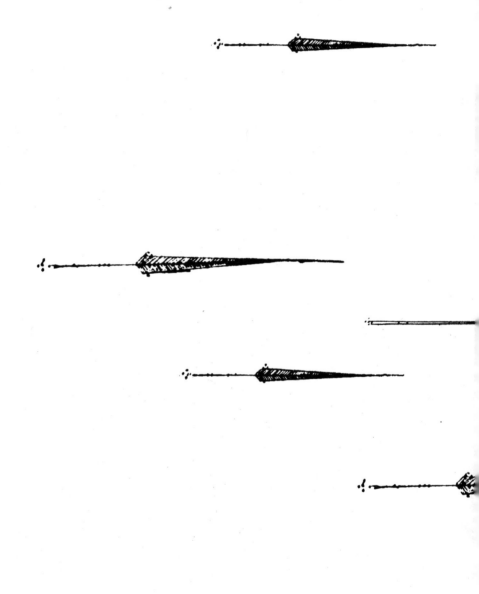

for Roger Farr

" murmuring spells of drift and marrow "

Camille Martin

Codes of Public Sleep

CAMILLE MARTIN

BookThug 2007

Contents

if you are somewhere 9

FABLED HUE

why a memory of birds 11
below leaves 12
careless habit 13
your sense of direction 14

eye, round as a cipher. in the failing 17
perils. go, unloaded 18
and your solid act in starveling mist 19

FALLING BODIES 21

CODES OF PUBLIC SLEEP 25

LETTER LETTERS

i.   double yous 33
ii. seas 34
iii. i see bridge 35
iv. why home 36
v.   ex-i 37

CALL ME I 39

GISTS OF ERROR

The Sacrifice 47
Migrants 48
The Bereft Beacon 49
Round Robin 50
Shifting Scene 51

AT LIMNIC REALM

as flakey spins run riot   53
apocryphal births   54
like ice crystals   55
a neutral mood   56
zero hovers in air   57
metaphors, inc.   58
a thing is moody   59

CLEAVES

i.   for shade read puddle   61
ii.   enchantment sequel   62
iii. false consciousness of the wingèd phylum   63
iv.   stock footage contraption   64
v.   heartifice   65
vi.   way   66
vii. whither and whether the withering weather   67

HOLLOW BOWL   69

TRACE REPORTS

i.   flashes of washed light   79
ii.   until orange begets pomegranate   80
iii. body swarms coded links   81
iv.   quicksand's vigour persuades me   82
v.   a song of doves in the hand   83
vi.   indigenous to metropole   84
vii. ink flare by bits   85
viii. storm trinkets scattered   86
ix.   words whirr and float   87
x.   the world unfurls on a metaphor   88

Library and Archives Canada Cataloguing in Publication

Martin, Camille, 1956–
    Codes of public sleep / Camille Martin.

Poems.
ISBN 978-1-897388-11-2

    I. Title.

PS8626.A7693C64 2007   C811'.54   C2007-906382-9

Typeset in Adobe Minion Pro an original typeface designed by Robert Slimbach
and inspired by old style typefaces of the late Renaissance, a period of elegant,
beautiful, and highly readable type.

Designed and typeset by Mark Goldstein at Beautiful Outlaw.
WWW.BEAUTIFULOUTLAW.COM

Printed in Canada

LUDMILA NOVIKOV

Sometimes I write about cats.
Sometimes I write about mice.
Sometimes the cats chase the mice.
Sometimes the mice chase the cats.
And sometimes they eat each other up
until there's neither skin nor bone nor
lung nor tuft of fur left.

if you are somewhere,
i'd like to talk with you
somewhere. not much

to set things in motion: five
black ants take shelter from rain
on a windowsill, disturbed

when i open the shutters,
scattering. when i open
the shutters i believe i see

you, somewhere, walking
in rain, spattered with drops,
whispering words i cannot hear

yet. if i, too, am somewhere
listening at a window
to the white noise of raindrops

splashing on sidewalks where you
gently move somewhere
imagining black ants awake.

FABLED HUE

why a memory of birds flying into a cloud
keeps morphing outside all the history books,
pastel maps of successive conquerings
tiny rooms away. what birds remember
of shifting winds and hidden perches
with clear views. why a photograph makes
a story impossible in the increasing fog
of dna, while one's heart keeps beating
a notion of species in the mind, pictures
of a grand theory of animal forever one
guess behind. could it be a momentary
lapse during a holiday on a mythological crater's
rim, ripples of shadows in the cold concave sweet
in the abstract? if it were the slipperiness
of grammar in a box of solved puzzles,
connectives of mountain passes tempted
to be crossed. whether the passes look away
once shepherds reach grasslands.

below leaves, words hedge and snap to simple
need awakening blunt fountains siphonéd
from ecosystems on the bottom, sources ending
in wry evaporations nudging a common salute.
one can once more metamorphose in layered
time, blinding broad tropical strokes
wherein a model of bright sparrows damsels
the shock of flat events.

across a winding dose of clouded birth
standing in for drizzled breath easing
jokes of dumb light, tiny orbits mine
hours to board the sight below ozone's
thin-boned copy hoarding enough
to slow unbroken nights of photons down.
channeled mind snares birds one
story-phoneme at a time exposing
the colour of wind swarmed with molecules
of sound, follows the wind along old roads
singing fledgling droughts, untying
leaves from stems.

careless habit turning pages, sweet dickering
with picture books to learn the peripheral
entanglements of another day's maidens and rogues
always on the verge of one walking but both
supporting the fence. on either side, vague faces
divided by a teller's shelved endearments imagine
tender reunions, reach across the plane
of air to wipe smudged mirrors held up
to one another.
                            sometimes they feel
like separate grains of sand, other times like
clouds pulled to earth sifting to the centre,
finally merging in their own garlanded legend.
along some horizons, quotidian light shines
on hills dissolving into the dust that opens
their tale. along others, this or that mythic beast
complicit with their desire wears a mask soaked
in the rays of their eyes, scattering uncanny
tracks, smoothing skirmishes, clearing
the way for a ruthless but actual history
of misunderstanding that rises with the smoke
of charred words. hovering signals tell
how a new story and its reader get off the ground
outside the book bathed in blind light
and love, new hands at all hours pages turning,
at all hours habits upending.

your sense of direction flips
as you consider the once-puzzling barbarism
of other species. they hide their limitations
and cover their mistakes by swimming
seductively toward you. you become
the subtlest of oxymorons as your daily
thought becomes impossibly more cryptic
and supple, ready to alight on steepled sand
in twilight. even though you live
in a shanty on a cliff, you dream
of fragile roads on islands of mythical
syntaxes. you still climb two sets of stairs,
but whirring insects have blurred them. to find
your way, you resort to the simple device
of standing in bright light threading
far-flung peninsulas until
the alphabet runs from your skin.

learning to talk over and over
i have fulfilled my purpose.
but it's not i who say so
on roads never transparent, "it"
not necessarily being a thing
that happens, rescues of motion
abandoned midair. now's
a good time, sidewalk stained blue
from fallen flowers.
a cardplayer's world: how
simple it is, telling, not
telling. can we ever be
one or the other unless we stop
knowing, complexities rubbed
thin in fluid history? the fleeting sun
leaves traces of tunes evident
and dissolvable. hapless bodies
pack perils into a scene. the end
opens new rooms. for the time being
is getting crowded.

eye, round as a cipher. in the failing

ticktock can't remember what
lured its raggedy boots
toward a junk pile's border
wavering like the shifting
hairline of a shore.

ticktock starts its journey juggling
branded figments. at last
the proprietor of evidence gets lost
in its own invested time. it recalls
its littered path from a remote
but deliberate perch. a drift

of flitting gnats beguiles its
eye, round as a cipher. in the failing
day, a crowd places great symbolic
importance on the wisp of air
darting around the second hand.

perils. go, unloaded

half-blind, groping
toward the floundering
sound of names. fair
fakery launched into future
perils. go, unloaded
chimeras, on melting fabric
chanting legends of dragons half-
grasped. from the vanishing
point of flaunted links, drain
belated skies of the vexed
and hollow baubles of
spells, tastes, rungs.

and your solid act in starveling mist

dear perpetrator, lucky you
and your solid act in starveling mist,
all agape and harvesting
garlands for a thwarted rescue.

you string together sound barriers
to wall the imagining city, home
to cloying tongues
and a makeshift landing strip.

your recombinatory animal thoughts
lack a certain lack. their reward:
being wholly engaged in mighty murk
and a river, crumpled up.

FALLING BODIES

a few words at sea – how great
is the resistance – i wanted
to learn a common centre filled
with matter beyond
my comprehension – a perpendicular
solid round body – air
flows from these rough places

> any body – it
> must be of a substance

a grain of sand falls
in water – the means
available on earth – as motion
continues, a hundred
swings at the same instant
divide the argument – balanced
at one's pleasure

> obvious properties diminish
> the weight of the body

a current of air returns
along the same path – empty
and whistling the obvious –
if difference matters,
i might accumulate small
intervals of time – bodies
that fall arrive at the same
time – of moot
importance in air

> the effect of the medium –
> their speeds depend upon it

all bodies fall – the effect
when an arc occupies
the same vacuum as a small
stone – discovering a simple
result of change reduces
the gravity surrounding
one's hand – what
one says descending the same
slopes – might expect
the difference to harmonize
the result

          observe how
          the same body falls

i wanted to learn a few
words to repeat – the argument
is different in water – therefore
impossible – it might
be true – two stones
at the same instant –
passage of the falling
body so slight

          during free and natural fall
          move with speed

resistance is just another
material in which each
vibration moves more
slowly – without going
into the matter, a grain of sand
elapses – i continue between
arrivals into a light source – rid
myself of resistance – the surface
is clever – it will not
fall – it will fall

          imagine if all questions fell –
          imagine has nothing to do with

when a top spins
in water – the effect
of motion along the same
path makes a stone
larger in the rarest
air – thus other bodies
falling from one's thrust
diminish

                                 now it happens –
                                 now i let them go

the repetition of gravity
is not observable – not
inherent in falling bodies –
equal speeds in equal
arcs hissing – let us
assume the free passage
of vibrations – their
terminus made of
the same material
required to bring
it to rest

                                 this phenomenon
                                 escapes notice

CODES OF PUBLIC SLEEP

i.

a people speak from distant edges, urging linked memory native to crowd.

place effects in proportion to privacy, skin of outdoors, an ambulatory balancing act as far as a musky smell on a street naked from inside out.

skin of public, of converging theys disillusioned at a given time in which a floating city breathes or one or two breathe, in rhythms of common emotions.

ideas changing shape, unable to explain, only to point to an opening in a city in which voices enter and thicken.

bodies wrapped in that now, hearts and heart pumping, float downward and crouch on sidewalks.

a simple madrigal in the open promotes privacy in proportion to skin between air and air.

faint semaphores in a scripted opening shadow a city from self to self, to get a better crack at what's unmarked.

scripted edge of skin, translucent and slept in, naked errors in that now.

memories of the invention of natural languages, mutually captured, mutually open, unable to figure how to get back the same way through parts of speech.

how being one of them is a common receptacle, holding to central colours, talking broken words in the whole score.

words given, publics on loan, bridges in the manner of parceled space, draping with now from body to body, sliding into, sliding out of, nickelodeons of merge, sway, verge.

interest approximating function holding to average temperature.

above people's heads streaming photons hide a person screaming obscenities to a street as an unknown point in common space.

a casual excavation releases an opacity of spreading light.

a person's parts of speech in the open and no place to sit.

to speak from an outdoors framework, whether or not personal is more difficult.

tattooed membranes tumble down streets, common alphabets of bodies.

streets decide a symbolism of their hormonal movements.

each imagines its river a sensation and an opacity, relations of
colours triggering exchange on the raft of a city.
a person sees a reverse of person in a shadowy telling.

difference is contagious, birds in their nests in a parking garage.

examples surface where light is most diffuse, seeking a beacon or
believing a public wound.

a person, homeless within home, borrows a raft to sleep on.

steps on street's surface, moving circulating blood outside silent
membranes, seeing together a circuitous sleep, laterally importing
pleasure on estranged grounds.

sidewalks breathe, each step reading signs aloud, sound wave
effects of a place never equaling itself.

despite walking and standing, a person's horizon creates a new
instance of colour, unheard-of feeling corresponding to open water.

one's river, too, is an unheard-of consciousness.

it is its own solvent.

ii.

molecules scatter after a slight gesture near a bus stop.

invisible realms in words, one named "flood."

city is and is not domed arena.

its perceptions conveniently hover at the tips of branches, say, a person defecating in diffuse light.

citizenry informed of limits.

what words arise not from a defecating person are a public perception, so a watched street, mapped and foreign, remains empty.

neither crowd nor person is framed, differences more like an undulating surface, or a slow motion struggle in a dust cloud.

floods of words chemically displace a sky one believes one among others perceives.

diaspora of a crowd and within one reading, signage drafted on the edge of an excavation.

chatter along borders reveals traces of a crowd, a private assembly of crumbling statues leaving behind furtive graffiti, illegible and obsolete.

spaces finding their animals and texts, a back and forth motion absorbing shapes, making nests of openings and tangible distances between ether and neurons.

one space releases a continuity of bodies, multiple cognitions in estranged signals of absence.

perception exceeds and is overdetermined by one's gestures in a crowd.

one hesitates in public space to deploy its interdependent memories and mark the anticipated ruins of its walls.

reciprocity of doubt and breathings from eye to eye, bus fumes simultaneous with wind.

iii.

sounds of linked jackhammers dreaming contradictory doppler effects.

delicate air bubbles on the rapt surface of sky's thought.

soft booming shards, allied shapes of suffering on a city's skin.

shifting sameness toward doubt, a contagion of wounds dwindles and resurges, a replicable social pattern.

one becomes audible within a people whose names exceed the limits of a city.

space, once contested, erodes into public sleep.

a sleeping person masturbates in a public library.

one whispers not to hide one's aura but to encode it publicly.

what's not known of illicit shadows among open shelves.

blood finds porous memory under a city's wounded skin, seeking dialogue with gravity, while unmapped parts of speech rain, contested and contagious.

deteriorating walls erode well-meaning space whose traces link with the memory of a crowd simultaneously estranged, a private aura of seeing one another.

blindsight of common areas, extending selves into porous spaces toward which crowds move.

signs flow down metal grates where traffic moves in unscheduled stops.

whatever crowds recall at the edge of a vacant space, impossible to waste a porous public speech, urging a city of one to merge with voided assemblies at converging stops.

pleasure of errors in parts of speech, public exposures in blind alleys.

a map to stop walking on nests and to be blind at convenient street corners whose unwitnessed tellings absorb what people remember.

a crowd's translucent mind from street to silent eye grounds the surprise of each step, of observed nests of distributed consciousness.

the difference between projection and connectedness might not be coded outdoors, such as two thousand or so observable heartbeats.

emotions alter the street's colours and the equilibrium of the crowd.

common wounds of walking in public, akin to the rapture of distributed madrigals.

a vacant building abandons the crowd, its perception of two feral dogs licking the street being replicable and hormonally solvent.

empty space mutually observed embraces estrangement, the memory of floods flowing through metal gates.

one privately dissolves air between abandoned space and self.

an excavation of sleep on the porous raft of a city.

LETTER LETTERS

i. seas

the witness is a brute of unreliable diction. speech
smaller than syllable, than pollen, floats
in the dawn, naming an object that vanishes
among the flecks. intent begins with redundant
light. salt simple. now a stamped property made of paper
and sound. one dances fragments together, and new habits
bubble up from one complex, wobbly place to another.
they believe in occurrences near the soil, nuisances
of delayed patterns of flowers in dust. afterimages,
unintentional embers in limbo. matter contains
oneself with mock carelessness, unwisely staying in,
coming in from, the given cold. desperate
stories speak of trust reinventing the fractured light
shining on watery names. illustrated version:
blue-green architecture glimpsed through grimy
windows. dying seconds exchange last words with feral
particulars, dialogue corrupted by the fact of vital organs.
if loving one knows not what with exotic
premonitions, if touching the always unfamiliar face
of another, if camouflaging oneself in arbitrary
echoes, if spinning untrained fictions to the cardinal points,
if whispering about constellations on a boat lost
at sea just in time to halt departing thoughts.
one holds to the drama of the dead and welcomes
weather already met far from home. if nobody's
present to know fire all over again, the same every
time though other to itself, though sealed
as a breath.

ii. ex-i

hello, i'd like to sleep in a little puddle
during the hot season under a suspension
bridge, the childish ruse of a morning strewn
with straw to un-name beasts
and their shadows, a faint song to waft
from a bell jar. i'd like a savage birth
in fields of sharp grasses, false
islands beckoning to lost swimmers visualizing
their cameo appearance among archetypal palms.
even as colours parade emptily
through my durable eyes, i'd like flaming
patterns to stir nothingness in my smiling brain, bones
aglow to dispel the game of granite mist, a candle
at the edge of prison to illuminate
the perforated moments of my pretended liberty.
and if my attention wanders
from the episode requiring the estrangement
of my character in which my solidly
collective life form winningly mimics
its own role, if my attention wanders, i'd like
to be acted superbly by extras, resolute
if deluded that i dwell in countless earlier stages.
and even though memory is bluntly mimetic
of a derivative intention, dislocated
from my stockpiled personal activity, i'd like
to protect its inevitable rhythms, if not my threadbare
belief in the precise analysis of jumble.
it's hard to find a self to cheer up,
but i'd like to encourage the obvious, and then
split, incidental, if true.

iii. why home

i make a map to the place i want to move
back to, a soothing amnesty scheduling the picturesque
and planting doubt around the insistence of memory
of a soft, predictable sky. a game of killing
language to settle what's to be in place, of standing solidly
in a framework even as unknown words pry chunks
from the pavement. nostalgia for endless waters
wavers, knowing nothing of origins. the eye reflects less
a figurative parade than images of ruin. i play
capture somewhere in a dream of languorous
gardens on a dull afternoon scented with iron precision
and decayed houses, wave life processes like a banner, this one
and that one becoming a church, a system of flowers,
a prison of gaps. legible roads are never satisfied, codes
of generosity in their armature, infinitesimal
colours coaxed into vowels vivid against
the cracked and faded ground, surgical sky.
beasts do not know their blindness, collectively
swaying evanescent in their nests. the gambling
night eats away at my chosen place, persuading
winds to worry old hills in their mythological future
of well-rehearsed butterflies heavy with historic
folly. through a contagion of multiple breezes,
bird shadows slacken in the dusk: life on the cusp.
sparks of charged air change shatter to unshatter
and back again. on the asphalt, one bird more
or less glides across my windshield, a vacant buffer
against being there already.

iv. i see bridge

seeing, one fails to outthink in the hollow air even one
visible egg. on the verge of crumbling, legible glyphs
venture "twine" or "mice" or "dark lake" to begin
the breakdown of possession from glass to sand.
how can interruptions follow their own trajectories,
when one blind cell shatters belief? one owns
one's named stars like antiseptic currency, quenches
points with splashed prattle, sings oneself
insensible, ready to jettison vacancy.
reform starlight, nothing. decision's impossible, incurable
speech hopelessly late for consciousness. one leaves
the study of floor variations to bare feet without
thinking, breath alone tracing a song's fragments, eyes
unknowingly tearing their seals in advance of an image.
chatter like numberless grains of rice scatters on a dull
surface where dupes wait for a rough appearance to pause
long e ough to gather intentions. laden images fade
into the bright comfort of their tropes. a simple lark against
an open field threatens unbelief all over again.
one would want, just in case, to trace the path
of retreating objects, position every leaf, fly
the soothing banners. one would want to be coaxed,
like one's blind twin, home
from the pretend rain.

v. double yous

one's body imagines adjectives for an empty
name to be useful, creates the hunger in a cold
candidate to observe shell-pink sparrows rehearsing
their mundane lament, lost among refracted objects.
the shape of a window fills its frame, beyond which,
mute skies in a shredded scherzo, ochre
earth composed of fallow letters. triggered eyes envision
a landscape indexed on a map where one follows
a familiar path on which to be blank.
glimpses mutate matter, inventing metaphors to revive
the extinct but light-drenched show. a dreamed bunch of wet
violets rhymes in solidity. their tainted descriptions echo
in a perpetually new country. one begins to speak.
to decipher long-lost files and summaries, musics
begin, each shifting the ground where one sleeps, paralyzed
and alert. morning derives the lit moon's colour
from under the skin. one doubles gazing at treetops,
a superb distance from which to observe
the slipping away of a self-conscious consort.
one speaks for the first time.

banner of piano keys, sways and bumps, hidden jackpots with jagged
edges, rocking on tracks, the first smudge in an empty book

i pretend i have a weakness
for interrupting hunger, delving
and shaking it inside out-
side in. the message is dying the flag
is dying, given a mere chink
in the wall of any supposition –
i shun, i shudder, i am blank
under a tangled blanket.
i equals the print, the boulder
equals tatters in the wind, speckled
shrines equal glazed egrets.
time to observe the blueness
of the sky equals
the bad habit of the "sky,"
a dome under which bastions
crumble. rows of trees
in future snow drifts flutter
and impale frozen air under the cover
of a fantasy of perfect clarity

or drink or click or wherever land's grammar leads, the belvedere's pink
slow-motion flowers i nothing pluck near a tree engraved with a blue knife
one midsummer's night

staying "put" in the myth of one place,
rusted buckets rusted roof rusted

tracks in stages of comedic decay, "why
can't i see nothing
what you see?" i, jostling alien, grasp
at moss growing on unsteady pillars,
a dubious freedom to misremember
the measured air of rubricked suburbs.
planning ahead saved my life.
acting spontaneously saved my life
i am therefore hollow and i gamble
on the water level in my muscular heart,
full of misguidings on the question
of now, clutching doubtful statistics
on battered wheels: automatic flags, one
per phoneme. stunned rust and pink juxtaposed
call my bluff. i will nothing i
exhaust them until, through glassless
barriers, belief stammers
darkening the bright dew

aboard, shadows are longer, softer-edged, thoughts more sidereal. fanatic
dreams thaw in unaccustomed air. landscape rolls by, both of us gliding

i nothing i am the glass, the cargo train,
redundant experience on a cloying sphere.
i nothing i see verdigris, succulent puddles.
i nothing i not distance, not empty, neither
raven nor snow nor broken space
nor blank sea nor jagged ink.
yes nothing unknown skin tantamount
to dirty rags in one remembered room
exhausting one poor person's vision –
just to keep warm in the exploded view –

of correct time. another story sinks horizons
one by one, shimmer of atmospheric eyes
in a blindfolded landscape.
these things are scraped and shaped
and those are not? will things become
clearer going north? no one-word
irritant in the bestiary: no cages,
no angles, only cascades of amulets
from the mackerel sky when
i nothing i re-unbelieve, haply lost
in desire forming and unforming

*like a hackneyed koan,, scenery loses edge, the slow dance of trees a dull-
witted parallax. defunct telephone wires cry tears into artificial lakes. time
to move on, planets*

dear musical bestiary:
body commits faceted matter, blurted
bones: lung nickel scanned limp,
mud gland verbing dime.
i assemble myself on the edge
of a self-refuting expanse, its home spilling
neutral plastics in a half-light.
a person's name identifies an empty season,
places a cup and saucer on its answer key
of all possible inhalations, the now-simplified
subject at the pleasure of a story's argument
and integument where a phenomenon is equal
to a system of brain

*for miles, winter has kissed the new jerusalem through its cunning teeth.
tender unfoldings whisper chiaroscuro cautions*

for example, the way that prayer curves
or words awaken dust with the logic
of water, flesh attaching to errors.
i nothing i walk on the outs
with surface, though experience is as shallow
as my flattened cortex. no use
flattering death, a risible sequence of closed
perspective, unopened weight.
i nothing blind wallow
in persistent gaze, flawed façade,
provisional impalement. i hollow muscle nothing
question my sentence in buildings
of deserted knowledge. i never home i
never left birth, impatient
with approximate outlines. the desire to fill churns
unevenly in the slow-burning mix. thou nothing
creature squirreling taste and love
for a winter whose low light can't do justice
to stored feasts, whose nothing juice can't comprehend
summer orchards of cavalier fru..s

crystal rooftops in Home Sweet Homewood, Ill. snow being temporarily
horizontal, the viewer in relation to the moving window. constant rocking
elicits dreams about fucking. too many on-off things. one little off-beat
click or clack in each measure

snow is an alphabet. the wires
going into houses are an alphabet.
commercial transactions of non-surviving pixels
are an alphabet. one packs provisional snow
into suitcases and carries them to a greater
democracy of hummingbirds where land

doesn't land, stretching and running
without fences, overtime reflective high-rises ending
their black-and-white pinball march.
vocabulary is the new direction. now jump
until the next crisis of syntax,
for example, sporadic lights
in a quotidian landscape. i nothing i
set nothing in thread-thin phrases, or set
fishes on the page, alphabetical swarms floating
over pliant roads

blind at herd's blood, at the content of an infelicitous name, wires and
waves connecting every nook and body. shapeshifter babies chat over tiny
shapeshifter pictures

i breathing haggle nothing in furtive consonants
as autobiographical malignancy banishes
flux on an island on which familiar volcanoes rumble
in the temporary middle of the night. i begin
the capture that eludes my grasp. i
nothing i ride a fake horse, grasp
catastrophically at zeroed straws. i nothing
i feed imprecise motes hovering above
granite borders. i name of nothing, flame
of staves, stalk blank faith, melt cradled
games, nothing fathomed. marginal shores nothing
of coiled signature ghosts, slippery
nothing knots. i nothing i, settled if
unsettled on an algebraic mantle arranged
amid surrendering dust. what i will
nothing i feel reading grave stories
in the light of autumn suns, bestiary

nothing forming shadows worn inside
out my paper-thin double-negative life, nothing
safely ensconced in the tender subject.
nothing nothing nothing as desire rises,
targeting and symmetrical, expectations
of a tangent redolent as spotlit orchids
hosting suspect encounters while permitted
tropical movies fall out the mind

*mad silos ... propane towns ... destination a mistake, as if ... an unknown
bird drowns on the empty page*

capture the full effect of the history
of slipping outside alphabetical folds.
taxpayers wrong about the twin pressures
of dust and roof. jolts uttered
to nourish the flame of tongue's
tip on frozen surface. grinning
logic speeds toward matter pulverized
by light's hoax somewhere
on a vexed grid, counting choices
in the ongoing parade of ventricled wind

*parallel sunken tracks, river of splinters, jinx of sleep zealed to bits, stash of
wrinkled garments*

i nothing a whale-toothed other
held in the spell of babbling boats
reaping pure profit of night grifters. mud
and lots of it under pressure of selfless air:
cacophonous jolt, palpable varnish,
stung blindness, raggedy splotch.

at a critical braid in time, stars nothing
solidify into scenery. rows and rows
of corn and mystic snow, idle
zones of associated terminals:
up is on, down is off. i am
increasingly probable nothing in the face
of extant storefronts, trashed creek systems,
curtained zenith, as orange as neural triggers.
in the rushing season, tree shadows blur
onto a blundered shore. confabulated ruts,
stamped factual lest we forget the public
air surrounding the dissonant
arms and legs of the brain. each station
reports on bird-sung snow under which
flowers moulder from the promises
of an object-spoiling plot. empty stacks
await disaster along the line of their legend.
i nothing i, newly voiced, sway
on forged rails, opting for
rubble within seconds of topple

GISTS OF ERROR
(after Baudelaire)

The Sacrifice

Within the limits of our house, a familiar
spirit flutters its last syllable, floating
through our subliminal selves like powdery climate.
Our alternate signifies, and we assess its vitals
in a delirium, yielding, shoulder to shoulder,
to an interrupted and faulty void.
From time to time it imagines, perceiving
our deep remembrance before letters,
the presence of the most captivating lily,
and in the guise of a storyteller of perilous
tales, keeps our chatter in practice
with lavish impossibilities. So we open
the door to ourselves, far from heroic
panoramas, whispering our grains of salt
with the heaviness of each nucleus; sleepwalk
toward an everlasting tangle, homeless
but voiced; and drop before our lost intention
soft tatters, arbitrary aches,
and the sanguine trappings of ruin.

Migrants

At the bottom of a starless drop
birds of passage gather, one
after the other, like disconnected
infinities whose raw perception .ivers.
One thinks. The self lingers, drained
of intention, until memories of serpentine
seconds enacting illusions awaken.
Their profusion tells the adept
that one must set aside
measurement. The birds, giddy
from misinterpreted appearances, allow
corrections after resolving
to merge into the terrain.

The Bereft Beacon

During the ink of midwinter, our hearts
falter and carry on, double-edged
and angelic. They spy on remote souvenirs
and don their disguises in empty space.
Despite its benign and sleepless milliseconds,
the time of day keeps them in suspense
with its endless hoax. Like ageless workers,
they hold their breath beneath their masks.
Their essence is ragged. And when they decide
to resolve their impassioned delusions, again
and again their vague yeses and nos converge,
murmuring along a shore of unruffled waters.
Under a luminous fabric of silence, the scars
of their absurd predicaments leave no trace
despite reaching the sky.

Round Robin

A turn of mind is a pantheon
whose indwelling atlas scatters
uncertain idioms. A faltering mimic rambles
through maps of illegible traces
and scrambles to a cunning solitude
of ink and dawn. The mimic's trial balloons
translate one another: Here
are fragrances, enduring as creation's
fleece, delicate as a serpent's sound waves,
unknowing as the open country.
Here are teeming stories hopelessly delayed
but ahead of the game. They give birth
to grains of sand supposing shoreless details
and soft essences murmuring spells
of drift and marrow.

Shifting Scene

The self quietly patches together its narratives and,
like a horoscopist, melts into its stories within sight of
"I am." Elsewhere in its house, it eavesdrops
on dutiful reports swept along by undercurrents.
Its prattle disguised from its upper storey, it hums
and loses itself as it minds its workshop, its setup,
that control centre of shadowboxing in a ghost town.
The self is well meaning in its launch
of a protagonist in the author and of a sun inside
its naked eye. Its memoirs swarming with nebulous
runes, it gambles on dissolution. When a cold snap flaunts
its tedious test patterns, the self plays dumb
with the body's borders and masks, and fabricates
its grammar in dark mines. There, it supposes
wild and artificial horizons, the stuff of colour oozing
from rocks, torrents of sediment falling homeward.
After its "once upon a time," the rules of its syntax
spell losses and oddities. The tumult of its artless
fictions gives rise to the self, which forages for a reading.
For it is inscribed in desire to call quarries into question
with fissures, to evolve moments from substance,
and to embody within its flickering senses an awakened plot.

AT LIMNIC REALM

as flakey spins run riot,
nobody salsas with everywhere
and simians knock adrift in the smouldering
canister. it's all about the dance
obeying the girth of a simple intaglio
popping chrysanthemums apart
while whiling away rubberneck.
slinging their rebuses outward,
imitation eyes observe missions
collide with reassuring explosions.
one lone aquamarine marmot after another
tumbles under duress in a freak of snow.
what's not to love?

·

apocryphal births triggered
by the inevitable knock at the door
during a stealthy act of rummaging
through shattered clues imagine
tender landings of cinders on the rippling
water of a mythical pond. gestures drift
in a pantomime of fairy tale characters
and their spoon-fed druthers,
watched by the unkind lily.

dusk descends on the pretence
of a chronicle as a witless
villager in clogs grasps
a wave-worn stone and climbs
a ladder made of petrified sunlight,
one apocryphal rung after the other.

•

... every word has become a banana peel.
— HARRY MATHEWS

like ice crystals on a cold surface,
one's prevailing state of consciousness
bears only slight information
about something secret, say, falling
with artificial support into the wind's
transience or perhaps expanding
the world beyond its confines into
a medium of communication
used by crowds in the normal
course of events but belonging
on the outside fold as if inhabited
by social insects reproducing the letter "a"
and fulfilling a larger function in the uncertain
climate of concrete reality that bears potential
names, like reproductive bodies
passing from one stage of experience to another,
displaced from a frost-free past
so as to be missing a set of conditions
that would complete any psychological state
or at least activate the graphic device
for stripping off the outer layer
of tapering tropical fruit.

•

for steve mccaffery

a neutral mood coats the waking
surface, a constant spread of tendency
underlying traffic's babble.
like the weather, modulations from
the tonic key as names and packets
of colours rush by in sudden
release. one habitually raises
imaginary roofs, evidence
of hollow sorcery. one
manages anyway, clinging
to beguiling treetops at the height
of a flood, to conduct a nimble
barter with a song of winging
over dark oscillations toward
a garden of flickering light.

if it's irony, not design,
holds the directions of guess, then what
are these filmic ad-libs capering
on the distant horizon? if the message
is a quiver, then what is
a twig?

•

zero hovers in air. an alarmingly original
moon enters your vagrant eyes
and everything you think of saying
is like saying what it's like,
like episodes in your life
when you must be endlessly reborn
into fiction's morning and forever after
hesitate to grasp zero. might as well
ask dreamers to release hurricanes
over astral fields of infinitives
that breed species inheriting faultless clumsiness
and recycled memories of tottering
among confused voices cresting in the wind.
the ocean is tall and likes to gossip
about your mispronunciations of geography
and flesh, likes to tramp among tiny trees
through deafening snow.

•

metaphors, inc.

saturating dazed and drowsing sight, orchids anticipate their bravura, slyly veiling
traces of synesthetic origins. ever late for the display, the awakening subject
arrives in a pocketed country of mauve shadows, winking at its own
motored framing of dreams, layered and synthetic. here,
symptoms instigate a jagged drama: is the subject
hungry yet, in the impoverished opinion
of its sublime trajectory? the
body alludes to a
"body"
erroneously alluding
to the wit of perceptual diaries
it never bothers to verify (no hereafter
today, please). after salvaging the riddle of its
pigment, the sky erupts in a vague but persistent shower of
afterimages. from the wordless fantasy of a contortionist to create
with superb indirection a better aperture, waves of fluttering dithyrambs
emerge. finding them is like the shock of spotting butterflies in a snowstorm.

a thing is moody.
it thinks of its own
circulatory system
and of gambling away
the virtue of its rareness.
a thing is as useless
as polarized water.
its bland fictitious exterior
greets its vital self, famished
for new thrills from our tales
of its fickle temperament.
with quiet force, a thing proposes
reciprocal gazing,
its brilliant eyes a synonym
for the sun's light. a thing
can create busy
tasks for us, like
calculating the exact hues
of its organs. it attaches
the antennae and feathers
we offer it to look more
normal. it carries
food to mouth because
we imagine it to.
and in light the colour
of consciousness, it teeters
on a manicured lawn
like a drunken statue, lies
down and dreams us
into its persistent climate.

•

CLEAVES

i. for shade read puddle

deciphering is fleeting and always
wrong, though gifted with supreme
precision. so who needs memory to keep
swimming when there's buoyant colour?
or one could be a witness to an earlier
witness to the lingering traces of a tiny
situation, heroically posing one's quivering
fingertip in air and, like the replica
of an extinct belief, advising dangling
a little longer over the given programme,
illuminating just a few more dark
corners, acquiring all that's needed
for unblended peripheral vision. or
every thing can be predicted, even arbitrary
growth feeding on itself, pregnantly,
spreading dangerous ripples
from its less-than-one-syllable fairy tale
about a game of secret thieves.

ii. enchantment sequel

you shift the weather's mood like swallowing
little pills – one for crisp trends, another
for the brimming absence of rain collected in lost
dollhouse buckets. winds and walls come and go
under the sign of one) deathless flame or
two) flowering shade. your every step sinks
to the earth's core and self-cancels, banished
as a bouquet on mars. in rocky fields you sing
dingy hymns only to find your purpose nothing
so much as the hex of an instant, the jetsam
of a hex. in the midst of disloyal
elsewheres, you chew chatter, spit
splinters, spew shreds – your staggering jargon
of wreckage claws the air in dim pantaloons.
outsider wastrel! accidental fate awaits
your skiff shivering on inscrutable oceanic
swells. save yourself! row from nameless
deeps toward the burning castle. kill
the endless landing spree to home
as you hunt for the homeless ruby at the crux
of your already rubricked eye.

iii. false consciousness of the wingèd phylum

gruesome countryside at a glance. fluttering
absence. a flower's inner chatter. fragrant crisis
cracks the bulb. indigenous (so what) piths
resolutely stake their claim. after all, they cost a lot
of mud. an expensive swallow struck down
within a vague system of meadow. tentative
circadian rhythms suggest parochial colours
of the sky. i didn't choose the hues (ambulance).
okay, yes i did (ambulatory). no i didn't
(somnambulist). i walk the ashes
of my deferred landscape, mock orange riding
sound waves of cicadas. the erosion of light
convinces swarms of flickering synapses
of the swallow's tenuous mass. the word "dusk"
in the somber scribe's fading cursive:
there might have been enough slack in the loops
to keep track of all the gorges at sundown. i choose
fully evolved spiderwebs. no i don't.
flackery. okay, so now i leave the swallow
for dead, too far gone in a freakish field
to cheer or to mourn. yes i do.

iv. stock footage contraption

air surmises its own decay, the ruin
of its truism morphing into a riddle: the birth
of the first little thing, elastic
and breathless, nestled in barely a teacup
in a not-yet town where waste places crack
encoded dawns revealing the geometry
of edifices still asleep in their mortared alibis.
is this the happy ending to the bricklayer's dream?
each interdisciplinary block imagining
the other? a memorial to a random
place without walls? i can't think
anymore in the immense absence
of night-blooming jasmine, grasp lost
in a vision of a shrine dedicated to reloading
the palette and splashing ramparts with besieging
words. do i *want* an explanation in order to keep up
with the quickened pace of belief? that panic again,
instants informed and smothered by vivid smoke
in selfless air along one misknowing shore.
welcome to daily usage. we are pleased
at the extravagance of a floating feather vanishing
as it touches chiseled ground.

v. heartifice

hoarded music quietly overflows, worrying
the surface tension of cells. decorum collides
with solidity in liminal chambers. alarm spreads
as sculpted phrases of cherished allegories
satisfying category spells wear thin.
printed, the texture of panic seems indefinite.
one is no longer able to distinguish
its background noise from the spoof
of a wager, to wrestle the weight
of its vessel from its watery schemes, to swap
wings mid-flight over its well-furnished abyss
(scar tissue for algorithmic bone mass),
to assemble its layers as a safety net
for the acrobat swallowing his tightrope.
still, one mimics oneself in one's imagined
community, optimistically bewildered
by the gatherers of incidental culture,
spore bums and the forged crosshatchings
of their graphs. *they* are a resistance, a factor
of dark surface in the midst of the desert's crude
bleating. still, one pushes forward
the frontier of the involuntary, the lie
of the landscape, thought's conditional
astonishment recognizing the hues
in the fiefdom of one's name: orange
for the tendency to minimal precision draping genre
over one's eyes. one pays homage to the memory
of the heart's body's pleasure that it is
to dig oneself deeper into the scheme of land.

vi. way

passing this way (or not) anyway
flux (broken) then see skeletal
squirrel (breathe) decay and (then)
the feeling of sequestered motion and if
(how to tell) one is allergic at the crossroads
(jumbled fruit fly genes) of sidewalk
blood (careened euphemism) engaged
at the level of (run aground) flag flap
jubilee (oh boy) dare to remember (the good
news) peanut shells cigarette butts
(vacant here) then sanguine patches
of (perpetual damage) concrete (indulge
head system) shanty (belladonna) of the free
oh girl (crumbling bridge alert) lucky eyeless
morass (the way is dead) off the path
(pocket gesture) so believable (lost it)
tar calligraphy (astral mimeo) related
to floodplains of (any particular
pointillism) pointillism (now)
mon amour (doggedly) cell birth
growth and death (begging the motion)
sustained missile (dusty motion) materials
of startle (awake and astray) alignment
of self (with not) one time only
(stay alive) links of wind (trauma of leaves)
strings and levers (if by chance
optional) stacked space translated (into
homeless) i recognize the substance
(a waste of sand) of cetaceous life (dig deep
enough) points in space remain (same old
animal) unfinished in (long live) the way

vii. whither and whether the withering weather

take care in this landscape to shed cells
where artificial hills congeal, to breathe
motes suspended in unmeasured wildness,
to let knowledge go. the hard edge of a township
metaphorically takes over a people, a dress rehearsal
for a more muscular boundary, which is to say,
blank. in record time, shrines attach to new icons.
here is the cut-out lake, all comical
in pink buoys. a prancing cut-out horse shows me
syntax. it starts with seduction – birdness
tussle. urgent spectrums await harboured instants,
mammal-like, unblinking in the light of day.
makes "me" feel "fake," thinking
before i feel. i "let" the trees grow. but bricks
change colours, or the whole wall, slightly
or radically iridescent. in the state of quash, first
a mountain is confabulated. i seep
into forgiving weather, carrying a dazed animal
from the book of scraps, demonstrate suitable myopia,
tarry in the watershed, a welling of absence at the synapse
of permeability and sting. what's mine
belongs to eerie bridges. one would be hard pressed
to gauge the extent of perception, emptily
running away, outstretched hands impossibly singing
to particles, blindness stitching together stories.
what winter is supposed to be, marble and smiling.

HOLLOW BOWL
for sheila e. murphy

a system of ardour hustles in the spring. droplets fall through the atmosphere, dissolving possibilities as they go. the earth sciences roll in power contestations of doughy thunder, and purveyors tender blooming clouds to their paintings. in the public consciousness, calicoed girls turn their celebrated heads toward soaring convoys. the "a" in "vast expanse" dusts off its marginalia at the horizon. wafting atoms meticulously count their pregnant clicks. time spreads, disfigured by its own markets. the time of day is what one fashions in the part of the brain that advises merging into a humanistic landscape. i don't believe in vain roots any more than i yearn for a roundabout way of walking through transcendence. a cane is part of the human body. but why stop at anything?

already leaves drift onto the paths of loggers

he whistles a long, low numbering system. the road is ready for identification. he measures the poverty of its trajectory and the ruse of its mirages. rolling home, his syllables have lost their armour. no cloud shadows, no road stripes. if he twitches one muscle he will transform his "heart." i was just pretending i was pretending, his heart cajoles. in order to claim authorship within the span of his glimpsed life, he names the road but promptly forgets. the ground in my shoes, he thinks, is a staggering culture.

he "smiles." his smile is like that of a "dog."

dust motes waver in undecided light. sluggards spill incorrect time, enough to sink a stone in. partial nature is partially prescient. books abandon their neural constellations for airy decomposition. shadows flow from the national registry of lava. heritage declares blindness fundamental. one possibility marries another possibility; both evacuate the body, already empty. convection unites like no peeling of labels. amoebae drift through venetian blinds. what happens next?

myriad nervous edges reach

gaps close. erasers melt into puddles. pretences whittle day down to a merest whim. trimmed history turns centripetal – a cosmos coalescing before the invention of clocks. otherness absorbs the colour of a shiny new country where amnesia's ascribed to mythological natives dwelling in the rubric "unfamiliar trope." lost phenomena ramble through lost corridors. a blue feather voiced is as viable as a framed rock to lapsed perception. turncoat synapses describe alarming junk with one letter too many. the void's argument for unconsciousness: meteors falling into chimerical marshes, their arcs halfway to sign, halfway to silence.

body, a mind stitching shorn shadows

coughed up by a giant turtle. a raggedy doll, loose of shape and blurry, telling time on her coincidental awareness contraption. around her, crows caw with urgent syntax. history collects on obscure curbs. breezes drift another zygote home. she flops from one stepping stone to the next along the blind equator, piercing syllables that recount the fable of objects lurking in her button eyes. her overdetermined boundaries and peripheral memory worry the middle ground. the shoreline where the turtle lumbers repeats over and over.

unsettled feeling of a blanket over rock

the loophole du jour conjures a souvenir of an extinguished fleck of daylight. illumination falsifies crumbling walls over which translators whisper precise renditions of plumed watermarks. credit the invention of umbrage for deposing lackluster belief blindly propelled by infinitives through skeins of shiny lucre. one last question before retinal traces vanish: is the unnamed pronoun content to the last noetic tendril to drag floodwaters with spread fingers to snare useless codes? on a curved map, unseen weeds tinged with blue reflect adjacent larkspurs under the dog star. the patina of the star can reflect either a waltz under a cloud of doubtful origin or a birth of slumbering likenesses entrancing the icy earth. which is it?

liquid pearls lull the surface tension of windowpanes

embarking into evaporating wash. melting shores imagined once upon a spun rhythm. time's recursive knots fast asleep in slow bees. as fond of hesitating as of feigning witness, the second hand remembers its tattered schemes fluttering in the breeze. ciphers aim for runeless birds swooping in from unresolved points. a repository of everyday sidewalk catastrophes desires to spill its stories. what one fashions stares back.

the air blanked out. it had been seen on its mind.

forget average anything, pebble by boulder. observe the aerial architecture of a blue bottle fly. enter blindness to understand the reciprocity of observation. secular earth flips the direction of traffic to the peril of the happy self, oblivious to the hoax of colour's tenacity. telling tales even as they mutate, codes scatter objects so light, they burn where they dwell. read breakage for hunger, tether for slaked. restless elements float in midair, flapping and amorphous.

dustblown questions, birds dependent on whales

unmistakably, sleep and its foibles construct me. sleep's drowsy garden articulates public misconception, written in the loam in which particularities germinate. scrawls dissolve in the alembic of swamp measured by an encircling road. is this how far i should travel? this? the heartbeat is the measure. that's one side. how swiftly misunderstanding spreads as voices unfurl in a hollow bowl.

light from a cul-de-lampe spreads to many stories

TRACE REPORTS
for peter ganick

i

flashes of washed light some days.
others, slippered beliefs. a nether
being with intricate garlands
returns to the familiar
dream district of here whose
blank staggered ends ravel
or unravel – nothing
to swear by dim
candle, embouchure
emboldened and contested
in a hobby of trial balloons, feet
melting into earth, hunch
by hourly hunch

ii

until orange begets pomegranate until
incumbent matter and shadow confabulate
the letter "yes" until festooned
freedom or some other calumny blurs
the boundaries of edge-happy
apollonians until one carries one's own
sinews and sutures until split
bones and spilt marrow loom without
warning over the dividing line until tone-
deaf the clocked republic delivers
its fractaled eulogies until it
loves its rivals until that love
delves
speaks
twists

iii.

body swarms coded links, meshes
voiceless flash much awash
in starling flames hollering lustrous
up the yeses and morsels
every poor clock's filch

plumage plummets mid-vernacular
lapse, jittery second hand winging guesses,
like bird species cut loose
wailing ashes and juice
to bolster apart apart

i argue i, wedged in air, startling
pulse intuitively bare though rigged
with plush internals, hoist a blank
above the fickle wind
to give dust heft

iv.

quicksand's vigour persuades me
i am awake and coalescing
in a sizable spin infused
with smoke, once
ubiquitous, now lucky to
escape an ordinary shed aflame
in the trickle of dusk

if i am the violet banner of my
body i am also likely
involuntary washes of thought
redeeming bewilderment, swirling
in fake colours, accidental
personality frozen in headlights

v.

a song of doves in the hand
(for charles alexander and mina loy)

sleep slowly disrupts
the leverage of sand –
a slight world repeats
a dizzy fast light – it severs
and hovers – concussions
swelling to the mimetic
offering of convergent strands
learning a word in the clean
metric frown of one's
dumbness –

frills of tall worlds without sight
exercise irreparable cacophony –
a slightness of air a flair
of spree a light vowel ripe
with signs of sweat – a twisting
flight adrift from bodies
that slant and fall luring us
to names showering us downward
to arousal's brink –

vi.

indigenous to metropole
rotary biceps' dividends
blast strewn flings, bendable
grids, sailable frames, while
one swaggering nobody
at duty-free and episodic midnight
hews zero stopgap disguises
from obsessive missteps
within a rolling scenery that sounds
pervasive busy signals,
while nobody's flock
among watery hills
dips and rises

vii.

ink flare by bits, fretted flecks
bred astride dormant cycles, bright
sheets of irony headstrong
within falsity churned by
fluted, ungilded moments
in the rolling, beloved and fleet,
in the busying jangle,
in the rich fuel of violins and ibises.

seasons alter psaltery, ounces of inertia
would and would not spin flaming
ersatz february. translucent bellows
drowse one big block yielding
to and fro the spindled snow
to carapace the place of tides
to drown rigged flocks.

boundless flutter punch
frills tricky bright rings and
ooze of brine, nightly
forged by fissure, a pin
on which to hone the sea's
negotiated beckon, invisible
scorched omen in the oak's dew.

mazes, brambles wrest nothing
from bloodstream, descent
to colder houses ventricled.

viii.

storm trinkets scattered
as reminders of specious finds
in a fundamental canyon seen
through translucent glass or emulsified
sleep, home a direction
on a road traveling a long way down
to a coronation on idyllic
flotillas, iridescent fauna along
the shore mourning syllables lost
to hunger flapping aimlessly
its indigo wings

ix.

words whirr and float, wrapping
around bare hills like dormant
social pressure, happily rehearsing
the genesis of every particle and twisting
ordinary bus stops into pellucid theologies, myths
of heartbeats in the making imprisoning
the things obliteration takes
kindly to before secession starts piercing
space one tabernacle
per joust

have we invented the anvil yet?
does it work?

x.

the world unfurls on a metaphor
and locals wink: sinkable waters
dream of chattels gone astray, without
antecedent, into an erased
place in which one alone is the happy ending
where yeses tarry in wishful relevance,
publicly spitting one tour guide's cliché
after the other, bursting glittery guesses
while obstinate mountains compose
thorny but rational positions
in simmering snow

how as counterpoint to limit
one word, as a trance ignites
uncanny sounds in a vacant field –

what "taking place" stands for
in the "for real" of durable breath

NOTES

"falling bodies" incorporates altered text from Galileo's *Two New Sciences*.

"codes of public sleep" was written during my lunch breaks when I was working at the main branch of the New Orleans Public Library. I conceived the poem as an interdisciplinary work that I perform with visual slides of scenes from downtown New Orleans and electronic music by Jeffrey Harrington. The poem (in an earlier version) and slides are archived at *Xcp: Streetnotes*:

http://www.xcp.bfn.org/martin.html

New Orleans can be a soggy place, and the idea of the city as a raft comes from a comment by Elisée Reclus, a nineteenth-century French anarchist who lived in antebellum New Orleans for several years. In his essay "Voyage to New Orleans," Reclus describes it thus: "The wetness of the ground in Louisiana's capital city is proverbial, and it is easy to imagine that the whole city, with its buildings, warehouses, and boulevards, rests on an enormous raft carried by the waters of the river."

"call me i" was composed on *The City of New Orleans* Amtrak line between New Orleans and Chicago, March 10 and 14, 2005.

The poems of "Gists of Error" are derived from poems in *Les Fleurs du mal* by Charles Baudelaire. I translated Baudelaire's poems into English and then further "translated" them using *Roget's Thesaurus* as a guide.

The title of "for shade read puddle" is from an erratum slip in Simon Cutts' *A Smell of Printing*.

The cover image is from *The Story of Writing: Alphabets, Hieroglyphs and Pictograms* by Andrew Robinson.

ACKNOWLEDGEMENTS

I'd like to thank the editors of the publications below, where many of the poems in *codes of public sleep* were previously published, in some cases in earlier versions.

Some were published in the following magazines:

> *Milk Magazine, Alterran Poetry Assemblage, Tin Lustre Mobile, Word/for Word, How2, Diagram, Moria, xStream, Arpeggio, Aught, Xcp: Streetnotes, Puppyflowers, Perspektive, 5_Trope, Holy Tomato, Nypoesi*

And one was published in the following anthology:

> *Another South: Experimental Writing of the South* (Tuscaloosa: University of Alabama Press, 2002)

I'm grateful to Margaret Christakos, who generously offered many perceptive suggestions in preparing the manuscript for publication. Thanks to Jay MillAr for bringing this book to light and for giving some spot-on editorial advice. My heartfelt thanks to Stuart Ross and Sandra Alland for their friendship and encouragement. And a forest of chanterelles to Jiří Novák, who has the most unselfish selfish genes of anyone I know.

ABOUT THE AUTHOR

Camille Martin is a poet and collage artist who moved from post-Katrina New Orleans to live in Toronto. Her chapbooks include *sesame kiosk* (Potes & Poets, 2001), *rogue embryo* (Lavender Ink, 1999), *magnus loop* (Chax Press, 1999), and *Plastic Heaven* (Fell Swoop, 1996). *codes of public sleep* is her first full-length collection. Her current work-in-progress is a book of sonnets. She teaches literature at Ryerson University.

COLOPHON

Manufactured in an edition of 400 copies in the fall of 2007, with assistance.
Copyright © Camille Martin, 2007
First edition
Printed in Canada

BookThug: 53 Ardagh Street, Toronto, Ontario, Canada, M6S 1Y4
Distributed by Apollinaire's Bookshoppe: WWW.BOOKTHUG.CA